HILARIOUS JOKES
FOR

YEAR OLD KIDS

A Message From the Publisher

Hello! My name is Hayden and I am the owner of Hayden Fox Publishing, the publishing house that brought you this title.

My hope is that you and your young comedian love this book and enjoy every single page. If you do, please think about **giving us your honest feedback via a review on Amazon**. It may only take a moment, but it really does mean the world for small businesses like mine.

Even if you happen to not like this title, please let us know the reason in your review so that we may improve this title for the future and serve you better.

The mission of Hayden Fox is to create premium content for children that will help them increase their confidence and grow their imaginations while having tons of fun along the way.

Without you, however, this would not be possible, so we sincerely thank you for your purchase and for supporting our company mission.

Sincerely,
Hayden Fox

I started writing a story about a broken pencil.
But I gave up because it was pointless.

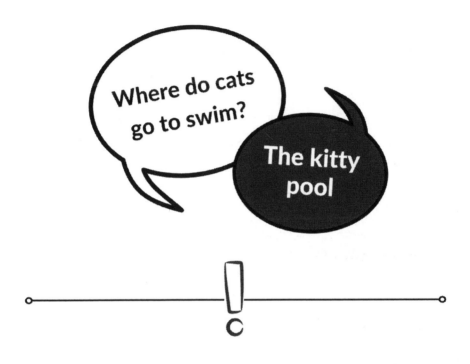

DID YOU KNOW?

There are 2,000 thunderstorms on Earth every minute.

The footprints on the moon will be there for at least 10 million years.

RIDDLES

I give milk and I have a horn, but I'm not a cow. What am I?

A Milk Truck

I am full of keys, but I cannot open any door. What am I?

A Piano

If one doctor doctors another doctor, then which doctor is doctoring the doctored doctor?

TONGUE TWISTER

Who's there?
Dishes.
Dishes who?
Dishes me, who are you?

Knock Knock!

Doctor: You're obese.
Patient: Whoa, for that I definitely want a second opinion.
Doctor: You're quite ugly, too.

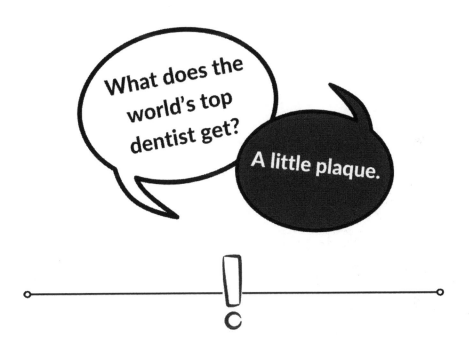

What does the world's top dentist get?

A little plaque.

⫶ DID YOU KNOW? ⫶

One million Earths could fit inside the sun!

It is a myth that lightning cannot strike the same spot twice.

Fuzzy Wuzzy was a bear, Fuzzy Wuzzy had no hair, Fuzzy Wuzzy wasn't very fuzzy, was he?

My body is usually made of brick or wood and I come with a lot of windows and doors. Keep me nice and clean for visitors and I will keep you warm and cozy. You can sell me when your family grows. What am I?

A House

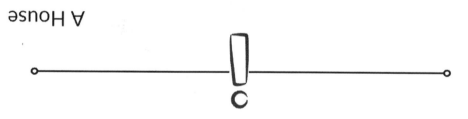

---: DID YOU KNOW? :---

The very first animals in space were fruit flies...they were sent up in 1947 and recovered alive.

Dolphins have been seen wrapping sea sponges around their long snouts to protect them from cuts while foraging for food.

Why did the teenager call 17 of his friends to watch a movie? Because on the poster, it said "under 18 not allowed."

What did the baby corn say to the mama corn?

Where is pop corn?

Who's there?
Alice.
Alice who?
Alice fair in love and war!

Knock Knock!

I hate people who use big words just to make themselves look perspicacious.

What did the duck say when he bought lipstick?

"Put it on my bill."

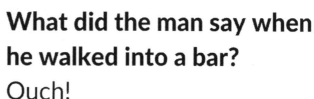

What did the man say when he walked into a bar?
Ouch!

Who's there?
Ben.
Ben who?
Ben knocking for 10 minutes!

Why did the hipster burn his mouth?

He drank his coffee before it was cool.

What fruit teases people a lot?

Ba-na, na, na, na...na!

-- DID YOU KNOW? --

An ostrich's eye is bigger than its brain.

You can't breathe and swallow at the same time.

Who's there?

Cash.

Cash who?

No thanks, I prefer peanuts!

She sells seashells on the seashore. The shells she sells are seashells, I'm sure.

What kind of bone should a dog never eat?

A trombone.

What do you call a rash on a pig?

Hogwarts

What did Harry Potter do when he went bald?

Got a Hedwig

DID YOU KNOW?

Cows get stressed when they are separated from their best friends.
(Cows—they're just like us.)

Can February March?
No, but April May.

Why did the high school girl only answer questions one, three, five, and seven on her exam?

Because she literally can't even.

Any noise annoys an oyster, but a noisy noise annoys an oyster more.

TONGUE TWISTER

Knock Knock!

Who's there?
Amish.
Amish who?
Really? You don't look like a shoe.

Why do pimples make horrible prisoners?
They keep breaking out.

⌁ DID YOU KNOW? ⌁

Octopi have nine brains and cows have 4 stomachs.

Hummingbirds can fly backwards.

Why did the picture go to jail?
It was framed!

What can you catch but not throw?

A cold!

Who's there?
Europe.
Europe who?
No, YOU'RE a poo!

Knock Knock!

Who's there?
Spell.
Spell who?
W. H. O!

Knock Knock!

I am edible, pink, and a great summer treat. What am I?

A Peach

RIDDLES

What do you call a dog that can tell time?

A watch dog!

⫶ DID YOU KNOW? ⫶

Clouds aren't weightless—they can actually be way over a million pounds.

The human brain cannot feel pain because it has no pain receptors.

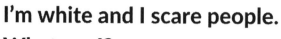

I'm white and I scare people.
What am I?

A Ghost

MATH
1 2 3

What is 47+11+82+161+99+5 ?
A headache.

**Whether the weather is warm,
Whether the weather is hot, We
have to put up with the weather,
Whether we like it or not.**

TONGUE TWISTER

Who's there?
Dishes.
Dishes who?
Dish is a nice place!

Knock Knock!

The boot black brought the black boot back.

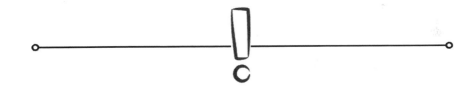

Who's there?

Mary.

Mary who?

Mary Christmas!

DID YOU KNOW?

Romans used urine as mouthwash.

Humans lose about 50-100 hairs a day

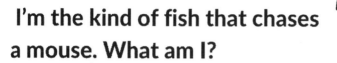

I'm the kind of fish that chases a mouse. What am I?

A Catfish

My home is in the water. You can drive me if I don't make you sick. Be gentle, don't put a hole in me, and when you're done, please tie me up. What am I?

A Boat

How do all the oceans say hello to each other?

They wave!

Where do hamburgers go dancing?

A meat ball!

What is a computer programmer's favorite snack?

Computer chips!

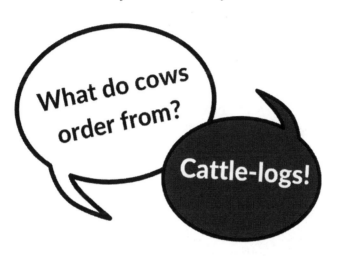

What do cows order from?

Cattle-logs!

Why was the baby strawberry crying?

Because her parents were in a jam.

⸺ DID YOU KNOW? ⸺

Before becoming president, Lincoln lost 5 different elections.

I get sharper the more I'm used.
What am I?

A Brain

You throw away my outside, then you cook
my inside. You eat my outside, then you
throw away my inside. What am I?

Corn on the Cob

Rory's lawn rake rarely
rakes really right.

TONGUE TWISTER

Twelve twins twirled
twelve twigs.

**Knock
Knock!**

Who's there?
Abbot.
Abbot who?
Abbot you don't know
who this is!

What did the microwave say to the other microwave?

Is it just me? Or is it really hot in here?

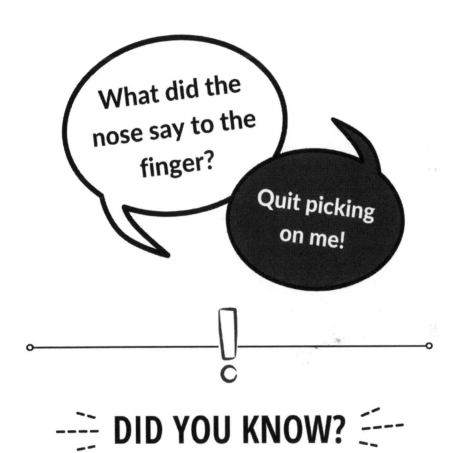

DID YOU KNOW?

You will get cell phone service on Mount Everest.

Ice cream was once called "cream ice."

I am a room, but you cannot enter me. Sometimes I'm poisonous, and sometimes I'm delicious to eat. What am I?

A Mushroom

What do you call a funny mountain?

Hill-arious.

A skunk sat on a stump and thunk the stump stunk, but the stump thunk the skunk stunk.

 TONGUE TWISTER

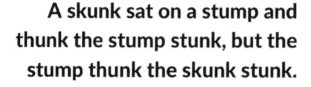

 **Knock Knock!**

Who's there?

Alfie.

Alfie who?

Alfie terrible if you don't let me in!

How do you fix a cracked pumpkin?

With a pumpkin patch.

I can go up the chimney when I'm down, but I cannot go down the chimney when I'm up. What am I?

ɐllǝɹqɯ∩ u∀

Who's there?

Some.

Some who?

Maybe someday you'll recognize me!

Knock Knock!

Who's there?

Snow.

Snow who?

Snow use. The joke is over.

Knock Knock!

--- DID YOU KNOW? ---

Women's hearts beat faster than men's.

Every human has a unique tongue print.
(Like snowflakes, no two are alike!)

The bottom of the butter
bucket is the buttered
bucket bottom.

TONGUE TWISTER

Knock
Knock!

Who's there?

Luke.

Luke who?

Luke through the peep
hole and find out.

How do we know that the ocean is friendly?

It waves!

Susie sits shinning silver shoes.

Drew Dodd's dad's dog's dead.

A synonym for cinnamon is a cinnamon synonym.

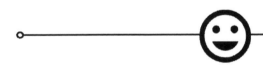

Who's there?
Stopwatch.
Stopwatch who?
Stopwatch you're doing and let me in!

--☰ DID YOU KNOW? ☰--

Most insects hatch from eggs.

Fred fed Ted bread and
Ted fed Fred bread.

Can you can a can as a
canner can can a can?

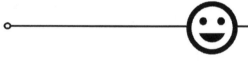

Who's there?
A wood wok.
A wood wok who?
A wood wok 500 miles,
and I wood wok 500
more.

Knock Knock!

Where do you find a dog with no legs?

Where you left him.

I have no legs, but I always run. What am I?

A River

I have keys but no locks. I have space but no room. You can enter but you can't go outside. What am I?

A Keyboard

Who's there?

Donut.

Donut who?

Donut ask me, I just got here.

☞ DID YOU KNOW? ☜

A hippopotamus can run faster than a man.

A crocodile cannot stick its tongue out.

Gobbling gargoyles gobbled gobbling goblins.

TONGUE TWISTER

Knock Knock!

Who's there?
Double.
Double who?
W!

What falls in winter but never gets hurt?

The snow!

I have four eyes, but I cannot see. What am I?

Mississippi!

I am a portal to another world which you cannot enter. Only you can see me, but I can't see you. What am I?

A Television

Who's there?

Saul.

Saul who?

Saul there is — there ain't no more!

DID YOU KNOW?

A shark is the only known fish that can blink with both eyes.

Little Lillian lets lazy lizards lie along the lily pads.

TONGUE TWISTER

Six slippery snails slid slowly seaward.

Knock Knock!

Who's there?
Dejav.
Dejav who?
Knock, knock.

What is a pony's favorite juice?

She really likes lemon-neigh'd.

Knock Knock!

Who's there?
Theodore.
Theodore who?
Theodore wasn't open, so I knocked.

Knock Knock!

Who's there?
Razor.
Razor who?
Razor hand and dance the boogie!

DID YOU KNOW?

Most people fall asleep within 20 minutes.

A woodchuck would chuck as much wood as a woodchuck would, if a woodchuck could chuck wood.

TONGUE TWISTER

Knock Knock!

Who's there?
Figs.
Figs who?
Figs the doorbell!

Please be patient, I'm new to the world. I cry a lot, please give me milk. Everyone smiles at me, please pick me up. What am I?

A Baby

What do you call a pig that does karate?

A pork chop.

If a dog chews shoes, whose shoes does he choose?

TONGUE TWISTER

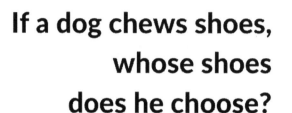

I fill up a room, but I take up no space. What am I?

Light

RIDDLES

Knock Knock!

Who's there?
Dishes.
Dishes who?
Dishes the police, open up

What animal is the worst at hiding?

The leopard — he's always spotted.

I'm red, blood pumps through me, and I live in your body. I'm the symbol for love, please don't break me. What am I?

RIDDLES

A Heart

⚡ --- DID YOU KNOW? ---

Your nose and ears will change shape
throughout your life.

Some tumors can grow hair, teeth, bones,
even fingernails.

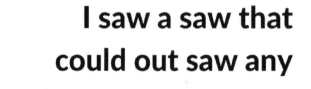

I saw a saw that could out saw any other saw I ever saw.

TONGUE TWISTER

Who's there?
Says.
Says who?
Says me!

Knock Knock!

How do you make a tissue dance?

Put a little boogie in it.

You use me to see inside of someone. What am I?

An X-Ray

RIDDLES

I'm the building with the greatest number of stories. What am I?

A Library

Who's there?

Leaf.

Leaf who?

Leaf me alone!

Knock Knock!

 **People think "icy" is the easiest word to spell.**
Come to think of it, I see why.

 Why can't you hear a pterodactyl in the bathroom?

Because it has a silent pee.

A big bug bit the little beetle but the little beetle bit the big bug back.  TONGUE TWISTER

Who's there?
Iran.
Iran who?
Iran here. I'm tired!

 Knock Knock!

What do you call a can opener that doesn't work?

A can't opener!

Why were they called the Dark Ages?

Because there were lots of knights.

⎯⎯⎯ **DID YOU KNOW?** ⎯⎯⎯

Arithmophobia is the fear of numbers.

Cat urine glows under a black-light.

I wish to wish the wish you wish to wish, but if you wish the wish the witch wishes, I won't wish the wish you wish to wish.

TONGUE TWISTER

Knock Knock!

Who's there?
Cher.
Cher who?
Cher would be nice if you opened the door!

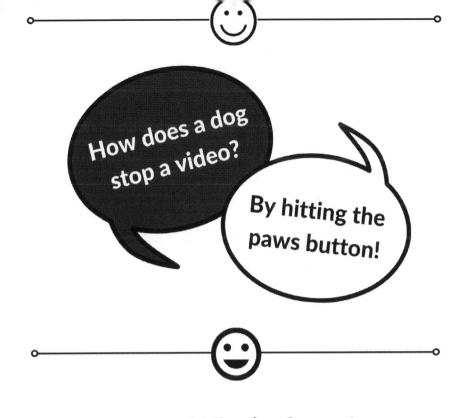

How does a dog stop a video?

By hitting the paws button!

Knock Knock!

Who's there?
Watson.
Watson who?
Watson TV right now?

Knock Knock!

Who's there?
Candice.
Candice who?
Candice snack be eaten.

DID YOU KNOW?

Fish can cough.

The snow on Venus is metal.

Hassock hassock,
black spotted hassock.
Black spot on a black
back of a black
spotted hassock.

TONGUE TWISTER

Knock
Knock!

Who's there?
A herd.
A herd who?
A herd you were
home, so here I am!

Boys: We rule because God made us first! God made you girls last!
Girls: Well, obviously God made a rough draft before a final copy.

People walk in and out of me. They push, and I follow. When they walk out of me, I close up and I stay waiting for the next person to walk into my life. What am I?

An Elevator

I am the only word that looks the same when spelled upside down or backwards (in capital letters). What am I?

NOON

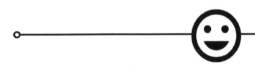

Who's there?
Kenya.
Kenya who?
Kenya feel the love tonight?

Knock Knock!

DID YOU KNOW?

Brown is the most common eye color.

Caterpillars have 12 eyes!

Who's there?

Nun.

Nun who?

Nun-ya business!

If two witches were
watching two watches,
which witch would
watch which watch?

My new thesaurus is terrible.
Not only that, but it's also terrible.

Two silk worms had a race.
It ended in a tie.

Who's there?
Hatch.
Hatch who?
God bless you.

Who's there?
I am.
I am who?
I am who is knocking.
Who are you?

--: DID YOU KNOW? :--

Kangaroos can not walk backwards.

Who's there?

Mustache.

Mustache who?

Mustache you a question, but I'll shave it for later.

Knock Knock!

The bottom of the butter bucket is the buttered bucket bottom.

Did you hear about the two guys who stole a calendar?

They each got six months.

I belong to you, but others use me more often than you do. What am I?

A Name

DID YOU KNOW?

Hippopotamus milk is pink.

There are 31,536,000 seconds in a year.

Knock Knock!

Who's there?
Cargo.
Cargo who?
Cargo beep, beep and vroom, vroom!

The thirty-three thieves thought that they thrilled the throne throughout Thursday.

TONGUE TWISTER

Sometimes I tuck my knees into my chest and lean forward. That's just how I roll.

If you have me, you want to share me. If you share me, you haven't got me. What am I?

Secret

What can make an octopus laugh?

Ten tickles

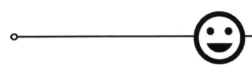

Who's there?
Keith.
Keith who?
Keith me, my thweet prince!

Who's there?
A little old lady.
A little old lady who?
Wow, I didn't know you could yodel!

If a black bug bleeds black blood, what color blood does a blue bug bleed?

I saw Susie sitting in a shoeshine shop.

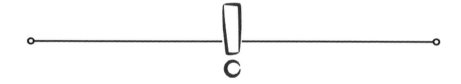

DID YOU KNOW?

You can buy square watermelons in Japan.

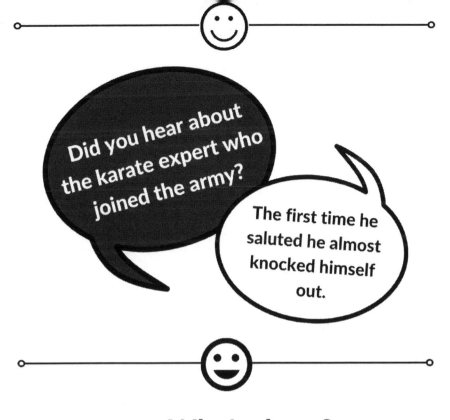

Did you hear about the karate expert who joined the army?

The first time he saluted he almost knocked himself out.

Knock Knock!

Who's there?
Hike.
Hike who?
I didn't know you liked Japanese poetry!

The sixth sick sheik's sixth sheep's sick.

TONGUE TWISTER

Who's there?

Manatee.

Manatee who?

Manatee would be better than a sweater today, it's hot!

Knock Knock!

Who's there?

Cows go.

Cows go who?

No, cows go MOO!

Knock Knock!

Betty Botter bought some butter; "But," said she, "The butter's bitter. If I put it in my batter, it will make my batter bitter."

TONGUE TWISTER

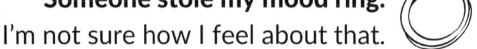

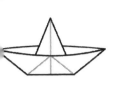 **I hated my job as an origami teacher.**
Too much paperwork.

Someone stole my mood ring.
I'm not sure how I feel about that.

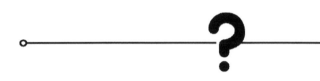

I'm tall when I'm young and I'm short when I'm old. What am I?

A candle

RIDDLES

You walk into a room with a match, a kerosene lamp, a candle, and a fireplace. Which do you light first?

The match

I'm red, but I can be green. At times, I might even be yellow. What am I?

An Apple

Who's there?

Voodoo.

Voodoo who?

Voodoo you think you are?

 Knock Knock!

Who's there?

Alien.

Alien who?

Um, how many aliens do you know?

Knock Knock!

Pad kid poured curd pulled cod.

TONGUE TWISTER

A sailor went to sea to see what he could see. And all he could see was sea, sea, sea.

Who's there?

Canoe.

Canoe who?

Canoe come out now?

Knock Knock!

DID YOU KNOW?

Vatican City is the smallest country in the world.

With me, the thunder comes before the lightning, and the lightning comes before the cloud. The rain dries all the land it touches, wrapping the earth in a blood red shroud. What am I?

RIDDLES

A Volcano

Who's there?

Dwayne.

Dwayne who?

Dwayne the sink. I need to use it!

Me: I cleaned all the dishes.

Mom: Aren't you going to put them away too?

Me: You have to upgrade from the trial version to the full version.

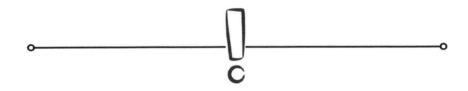

DID YOU KNOW?

Boys have fewer taste buds than girls.

How did the bullet lose its job?

It got fired.

Knock Knock!

Who's there?

Anita.

Anita who?

Let me in! Anita borrow something.

Five frantic frogs fled from fifty fierce fishes.

Chester cheetah chews a chunk of cheap cheddar cheese.

Who's there?

Knock Knock!

Annie.

Annie who?

Annie thing you can do, I can do too!

What kind of key can never unlock a door?

A monkey

How much dew does a dewdrop drop? If dewdrops do drop dew?

TONGUE TWISTER

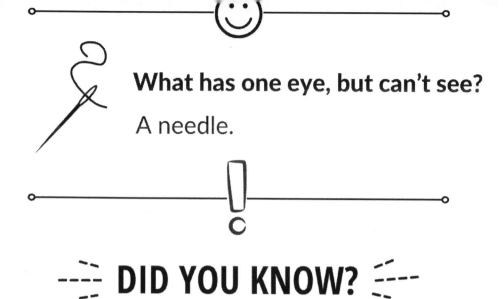

What has one eye, but can't see?

A needle.

---: DID YOU KNOW? :---

You fart on average 14 times a day, and each fart travels from your body at 7 mph.

I sound like one letter, but I'm written with three. I show you things when you look through me. What am I?

RIDDLES

An Eye

I am black when you get me, red when you use me, and white when you're finished with me. What am I?

Charcoal

Who's there?

Hawaii.

Hawaii who?

I'm good. Hawaii you?

RIDDLES

I don't have eyes, ears, a nose, or a tongue, but I can see, smell, hear, and taste everything. What am I?

A Brain

I am associated with spring and I love to hop around in the grass. I like playing in your vegetable garden and my teeth are long and sharp. What am I?

A Rabbit

TONGUE TWISTER

I slit the sheet, the sheet I slit, and on the slitted sheet I sit.

What stays in a corner but can travel the world?

A postage stamp.

What is a ninja's favorite kind of shoes?

Sneakers

-- DID YOU KNOW? --

Cats are not able to taste anything that is sweet.

Because bananas contain potassium, they are radioactive.

Where does fruit go on vacation?

Pearis.

Who's there?

Orange.

Orange who?

Orange you going to let me in?

Knock Knock!

Two tried and true tridents, two tried and true tridents, two tried and true tridents.

TONGUE TWISTER

What's worse than finding a worm in your apple?

Finding half a worm in your apple.

What do you call a grizzly with no teeth?

A gummy bear.

Though I am only two words, I have thousands of letters in me. What am I?

Post Office

RIDDLES

I twist and turn and leave a loop. What am I?

A Shoe String

Who's there?
Thermos.
Thermos who?
Thermos be a better way
to get to you.

Who's there?
Norma Lee.
Norma Lee who?
Norma Lee I don't knock
on random doors, but I
had to meet you!

**Wayne went to Wales to
watch walruses.**

**Lesser leather never
weathered wetter
weather better.**

What do you call a Star Wars droid that takes the long way around?

R2-Detour

Who's there?

Yukon.

Yukon who?

Yukon say that again!

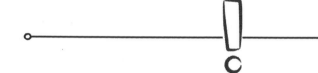

Knock Knock!

DID YOU KNOW?

When cranberries are ripe, they can bounce like a ball.

Antarctica is the only continent with no permanent human residents.

I spend the day in the window and I hide at night. When I get hungry I will visit your table for a meal. What am I?

A Fly

Who's there?

Pecan.

Pecan who?

Pecan someone your own size.

Knock Knock!

On a lazy laser raiser lies a laser ray eraser.

Six socks sit in a sink soaking in soap suds.

What kind of tea is hard to swallow?

Reali-tea.

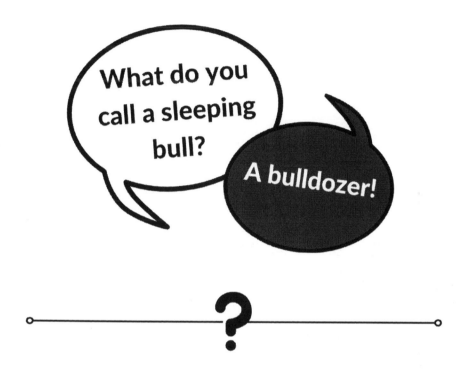

What do you call a sleeping bull?

A bulldozer!

I have two legs, but they only touch the ground when I'm not moving. What am I?

A Wheelbarrow

RIDDLES

You can serve me, but you can't eat me. What am I?

A Tennis Ball

What shows up four times in a teenager's life, once in adult life and never in childhood?

ǝ ɹǝʇʇǝl ǝɥꓕ (The letter E)

I'm a bird but can also lift up to 60 tonnes. What am I?

ǝuɐɹϽ ∀ (A Crane)

Many an anemone sees an enemy anemone.

TONGUE TWISTER

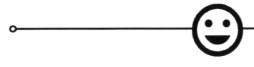

Knock Knock!

Who's there?

Ice cream.

Ice cream who?

Ice cream if you don't give me some candy!

What side of a turkey has the most feathers?

The outside!

What animal needs to wear a wig?

A bald eagle!

⟶ DID YOU KNOW? ⟵

igers also have striped skin, not just striped fur.

Koala's fingerprints are so similar to human fingerprints that they could taint a crime scene.

Who's there?

Knock Knock!

Nana.

Nana who?

Nana your business.

What has hands but can't clap?

A clock!

Round and round the rugged rock the ragged rascal ran.

TONGUE TWISTER

What does an evil hen lay?

Deviled eggs!

Who's there?

Sue.

Sue who?

I'll see you in court!

Knock Knock!

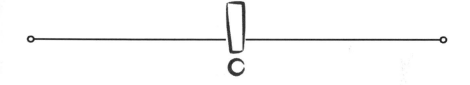 **DID YOU KNOW?**

Shrimp's hearts are in their heads.

A hurricane releases enough energy
in one second to equal that of
10 atomic bombs.

I never ask questions, but I'm always answered. What am I?

A Doorbell

The more you have of me, the less you see. What am I?

Darkness

Who's there?
Ray Dee.
Ray Dee who?
Ray Dee or not,
here I come!

Knock Knock!

TONGUE TWISTER

How many yaks could a yak pack pack if a yak pack could pack yaks?

How many apples grow on a tree?

All of them!

DID YOU KNOW?

The Double Coconut palm produced the biggest seed in the world: 45 pounds.

Knock Knock!

Who's there?

Sadie.

Sadie who?

Sadie magic word and I'll come in!

Who's there?

Scold.

Scold who?

Scold enough out here to go ice skating!

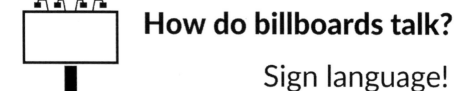 **How do billboards talk?**

Sign language!

I wish you were a fish in my dish.

Elizabeth has eleven elves in her elm tree.

Two pickles fell out of a jar onto the floor. What did one say to the other?

Dill with it.

--☰ DID YOU KNOW? ☰--

The fastest recorded raindrop was 20 mph!

Potatoes were used as currency throughout human history.

Knock Knock!

Who's there?

Isabel.

Isabel who?

Isabel working?

Who's there?

Mustache.

Mustache who?

I mustache you a question

Who's there?

Alex.

Alex who?

Alex-plain later!

**Old oily Ollie
oils old oily autos.**

**A big black bug bit a big
black bear, and made the
big black bear bleed blood.**

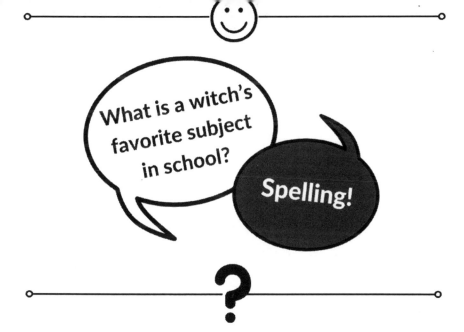

What is a witch's favorite subject in school?

Spelling!

Children love to play with me but not inside, only out. Watch out for the wires and trees for you could tangle me. Look up and watch me dance, the faster you run the faster I will too. What am I?

RIDDLES

A Kite

Cooks cook cupcakes quickly.

TONGUE TWISTER

Octopus ocular optics.

Knock Knock!

Who's there?
Imma.
Imma who?
Imma getting older waiting
for you to open up!

Knock Knock!

Who's there?
Sheriff.
Sheriff who?
Hey, I'm the one asking
the questions here!

--- DID YOU KNOW? ---

**Nearly 10% of all of a cat's bones are
in its tail.**

Why was 6 afraid of 7?

Because 7, 8, 9.

What do you call a boomerang that won't come back?

A stick

What do you call a ghost's true love?

His ghoul-friend.

What do you call an alligator with a vest?

An investigator!

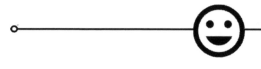

Knock Knock!

Who's there?
Shore.
Shore who?
Shore hope you like this knock-knock joke!

Three fluffy feathers fell from Phoebe's flimsy fan.

TONGUE TWISTER

Why can't Elsa have a balloon?

Because she will let it go.

I am a fruit that can talk, calculate, and tweet. It is well-known that I don't come cheap. What am I?

Any Apple Product

RIDDLES

Who's there?
Arfur.
Arfur who?
Arfur got!

 Knock Knock!

Who's there?
Ketchup.
Ketchup who?
Ketchup with me, and I'll tell you!

Knock Knock!

DID YOU KNOW?

A cat has 32 muscles in each ear.

The giant squid has the largest eyes in the world.

Why was the mathematics book sad?

It had too many problems.

Who's there?

Amarillo.

Amarillo who?

Amarillo nice person.

Knock Knock!

Who's there?

Utah.

Utah who?

U-talking to me?

Knock Knock!

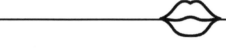

Fresh French fried fly fritters.

How much wood could a wood chuck chuck if a wood chuck could chuck wood.

TONGUE TWISTER

I'm not clothes but I can cover your body. The more I'm used, the thinner I grow. What am I?

RIDDLES

A Bar of Soap

She saw Sharif's shoes on the sofa.

Who's there?

Cuck.

Cuck who?

What, are you a clock now?

---= DID YOU KNOW? =---

Monkeys can go bald in old age,
just like humans.

Bees are found everywhere in the world
apart from Antarctica.

Why did the pirate have to learn the alphabet?

Because he was always lost at C.

If April showers bring Mayflowers, what do Mayflowers bring?

Pilgrims.

I'm pinched by Grandmas and Aunts. What am I?

Cheeks

RIDDLES

Say my name and I will disappear. What am I?

Silence

⌇ **DID YOU KNOW?** ⌇

Cows can walk upstairs but not down them.

Knock Knock!

Who's there?
Wooden shoe.
Wooden shoe who?
Wooden shoe like to hear more jokes?

Knock Knock!

Who's there?
Honeydew.
Honeydew who?
Honeydew you wanna dance?

What did one toilet say to the other?

You look flushed.

If you have 13 apples in one hand and 10 oranges in the other, what do you have?

Big hands.

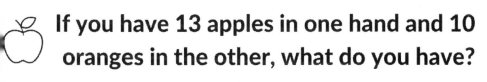

---- **DID YOU KNOW?** ----

Are you terrified that a duck is watching you? Some people are. That is anatidaephobia.

Knock Knock!

Who's there?

Robin.

Robin who?

Robin you! Now hand over the cash.

Kindly kittens knitting mittens keep kazooing in the king's kitchen.

Waiter! Waiter! This coffee tastes like soil.

Yes, sir, it was ground this morning.

Who's there?

Gorilla.

Gorilla who?

Gorilla me a hamburger

Who's there?

Tank.

Tank who?

You're welcome.

I wrote a song about a tortilla.
Well actually, it's more of a rap.

 A lot of people cry when they cut an onion.
The trick is not to form an emotional bond.

DID YOU KNOW?

Your fingernails grow slower when you are cold.

**Peanut oil can be used as an ingredient
to make dynamite.**

**I give people a huge fright, but
at the end I'm sweet. I'm usually
celebrated at night. What am I?**

Halloween

Any noise annoys an oyster but a noisy noise annoys an oyster more.

Knock Knock!

Who's there?
Opportunity.
Opportunity who?
Opportunity doesn't knock twice!

Knock Knock!

Who's there?
Art.
Art who?
R2-D2!

I am full of holes, but I can still hold a lot of water. What am I?

A Sponge

RIDDLES

Is this pool safe for diving?

It deep ends.

Why did the boy run around his bed?

Because he was trying to catch up on sleep.

What do you get when you cross a snowman and a vampire?

Frostbite!

Who's there?

I am.

I am who?

So you have identity problems, huh?

Who's there?

Police.

Police who?

Police hurry, I've got to go to the bathroom.

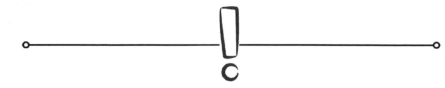

DID YOU KNOW?

You cannot smell while you sleep.

What do you call a Minecraft meetup IRL?

A block party.

Does your sport shop stock short socks with spots?

TONGUE TWISTER

When I point up, it's bright.
When I point down, it's dark.
What am I?

RIDDLES

A Light Switch

The more you take away from me, the larger I become. What am I?

A Hole

Four furious friends fought for the phone.

What race is never run?

A swimming race.

Who's there?
To.
To who?
It's to whom.

Who's there?
Boo.
Boo who?
Don't cry!

Why do rappers need umbrellas?

Fo' drizzle

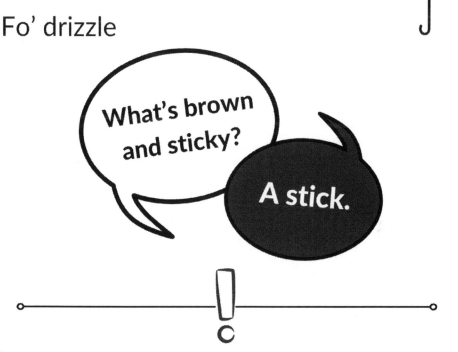

What's brown and sticky?

A stick.

--- **DID YOU KNOW?** ---

Most people cannot lick their elbows.

Your blood is as salty as the ocean.

We surely shall see the sunshine soon.

TONGUE TWISTER

Betty and Bob brought back blue balloons from the big bazaar.

Who's there?

You.

You who?

You hoo? Anybody home?

Who's there?

Horsp.

Horsp who?

Did you just say horse poo?

What did the French teacher say to the class?
I don't know — I couldn't understand her.

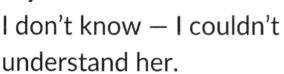

Give papa a cup of proper offee in a copper coffee cup.

Who's there?
Woo.
Woo who?
Ohh someone's excited!

Who's there?
Razor.
Razor who?
Razor hands, this is a stick up!

I go up and down at the same time. Up toward the sky and down toward the ground. What am I?

RIDDLES

A See-Saw

--∴ DID YOU KNOW? ∵--

Maine is the closest state to Africa.

Starfish have no brains.

Who's there?

Ivor.

Ivor who?

Ivor you let me in or I'll climb through the window

Knock Knock!

I couldn't figure out why the baseball kept getting larger. Then it hit me.

Knock Knock!

Who's there?

Etch.

Etch who?

Bless you!

Knock Knock!

Who's there?

Closure.

Closure who?

Closure mouth while you're chewing!

DID YOU KNOW?

One-quarter of your bones are in your feet.

Sloths are strong swimmers, especially good at the backstroke.

Leave Your Feedback on Amazon

Please think about leaving some feedback via a review on Amazon. It may only take a moment, but it really does mean the world for small businesses like mine.

Even if you did not enjoy this title, please let us know the reason(s) in your review so that we may improve this title and serve you better.

From the Publisher

Hayden Fox's mission is to create premium content for children that will help them expand their vocabulary, grow their imaginations, gain confidence, and share tons of laughs along the way.

Without you, however, this would not be possible, so we sincerely thank you for your purchase and for supporting our company mission.

Thank you for reading!

Made in the USA
Las Vegas, NV
15 December 2022

62851243R00059